MW01253961

 **ID9**

FAST-TRACK INSTRUCTIONAL DESIGN

Excellence in Course Development Using ID9™

CATHERINE MATTISKE

TPC - The Performance Company Pty Ltd
PO Box 639
Rozelle NSW 2039
Sydney, Australia

ACN 077 455 273
email: info@tpc.net.au
Website: www.tpc.net.au

© TPC – The Performance Company Pty Limited
Publication date: April 4, 2011

All rights reserved. Apart from any fair dealing for the purposes of study, research or review, as permitted under Australian copyright law, no part of this publication may be reproduced by any means without the written permission of the copyright owner. Every effort has been made to obtain permission relating to information reproduced in this publication.

The information in this publication is based on the current state of commercial and industry practice, applicable legislation, general law and the general circumstances as at the date of publication. No person shall rely on any of the contents of this publication and the publisher and the author expressly exclude all liability for direct and indirect loss suffered by any person resulting in any way from the use of or reliance on this publication or any part of it. Any options and advice are offered solely in pursuance of the author's and the publisher's intention to provide information, and have not been specifically sought.

National Library of Australia
Cataloguing-in-Publication data

Mattiske, Catherine
Fast-track Instructional Design: Excellence in Course Development Using ID9

ISBN 978-1-921547-06-5

  1. Occupational training   2. Learning   I. Title

370.113

Printed in USA

Distributed by TPC - The Performance Company - www.tpc.net.au
For further information contact TPC - The Performance Company, Sydney Australia on +61 9555 1953 or
TPC - The Performance Company, California on +1 818-227-5052, or email info@tpc.net.au

HELLO.

Welcome to the Learning Short-take® process!

This Learning Short-take® is a bite sized learning package that aims to improve your skills and provide you with an opportunity for personal and professional development to achieve success in your role.

This Learning Short-take® combines self study with workplace activities in a unique learning system to keep you motivated and energized. So let's get started!

Step 1:
What's inside?

- Learning Short-take® Participant Guide. This section contains all of the learning content and will guide you through the learning process.
- Learning Activities. You will be prompted to complete these as you read through the Participant Guide.
- Learning Journal. This is a summary of your key learnings. Update it when prompted.
- Skill Development Action Plan. Learning is about taking action. This is your action plan where you'll plan how you will implement your learning.

Step 2:
Complete the Learning Short-take®

- Learning Short-takes® are best completed in a quiet environment that is free of distractions.
- Schedule time in your calendar to complete the Learning Short-take® and prioritize this time as an investment in your own professional development.
- Depending on the title, most participants complete the Learning Short-take® from 90 minutes to 2.5 hours.

Step 3:
Meet with your Manager/Coach

- Schedule a 30 minute meeting with your Manager or Coach.
- At this meeting share your completed Activities, Learning Journal and Skill Development Action Plan.
- Most importantly, discuss and agree on how you will implement your learning in your role.

Welcome

Fast-track Instructional Design
Excellence in Course Development Using ID9

Fast-track Instructional Design combines self-study with real workplace activities to provide you with loads of tips, tricks and techniques for writing and creating sensational training courses. You will learn Mattiske's ID9™ process that reduces instructional design time, balances the needs of all learners, and ensures maximum participant retention and application. ID9™ will fuel you with new ideas and recharge your enthusiasm for course design.

A sound instructional design process is critical to training success and learning retention. The instructional design process dictates the flow of the training program and, if structured effectively, ensures both trainer and participants achieve program and learning objectives. **Fast-track Instructional Design** introduces ID9™, the 9-step instructional design model, which facilitates program success from a 'great Open' to a 'sensational Close.'

Fast-track Instructional Design includes the **ID9™ Wallchart**, provided as a free downloadable tool.

Now let's get started!

"Anyone who stops learning is old, whether at twenty or eighty."

Henry Ford

"There are precious few Einsteins among us. Most brilliance arises from ordinary people working together in extraordinary ways."

Roger Von Oech

Section 1

PARTICIPANT GUIDE

Start here

What's in this Participant Guide

"You can teach a student a lesson for a day; but if you can teach him to learn by creating curiosity, he will continue the learning process as long as he lives."

Clay P. Bedford

Table of Contents

How to complete your Learning Short-take®

1. Reflect on your skills and abilities in understanding how adults learn, and how you use this information to improve effectiveness in your role.

2. Complete the Activities as directed.

3. Highlight specific skill areas that you believe you could develop more. Add these to the Learning Journal. Add to your Learning Journal as you go.

4. When you have completed this Learning Short-take® meet with your Manager/Coach. In this meeting, you will jointly establish a personal Skill Development Action Plan.

5. Subject to your coach's final review and assessment, you will either sign off the module, or undertake further skill development as appropriate.

"Professors known as outstanding lecturers do two things; they use a simple plan and many examples."

W. McKeachie

Activity Checklist

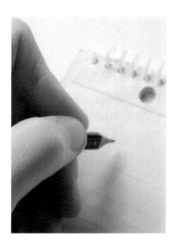

"No one is ready
for a thing unless
he believes he can
acquire it. "

Napoleon Hill

During this Learning Short-take® you will be prompted to complete the following activities:

Pre-requisite Checklist

Participants should have completed or have prior knowledge of:

- **The Learning Short-take®:**
  Adult Learning Principles 1
  – Engaging the Adult Learner

If you do not have this pre-requisite discuss this with the person who asked you to complete this self-directed learning project, or complete the pre-requisite yourself.

"Learning is a treasure that will follow its owner everywhere."

Chinese Proverb

Learning Objectives

"All the world is a laboratory to the inquiring mind."

Martin H. Fischer

Once you have completed this Learning Short-take®, you should be able to:

- Write clear and concise course goals.

- Write results oriented learning objectives using action verbs.

- Demonstrate practical use of the 9-step Instructional Design ID9™ model in course development.

- Create a smooth-flowing session opening, including the Welcome, Icebreaker, Agenda, Objectives, and Connect Activity.

- Work with all types of content and create interactive learning sessions with sound adult learning processes.

- Design training that will ensure participant interaction.

- Write effective review activities and closing phase to all training.

- Create a Skill Development Action Plan.

Let's Get Started

A sound instructional design process is critical to training success and learning retention. The instructional design process dictates the flow of the training program and if structured effectively, ensures both trainer and participant achieve program and learning objectives. This Learning Short-take® introduces the 9-step instructional design ID9™ model to facilitate program success from a "great Open" to a "sensational Close".

This Learning Short-take® combines self-study with workplace activities to provide you with loads of tips, tricks and techniques for writing and creating effective training courses. You will learn a proven 9-step process which reduces instructional design time, balances the needs of all learners, and ensures maximum participant retention and application. It will fuel you with new ideas and recharge your enthusiasm for course design.

The Learning Short-take® is designed for completion in approximately 90 minutes.

"The mind, once stretched by a new idea, never regains its original dimensions."

Oliver Wendell Holmes

Task # 1 - Choose your content

During this self-directed learning project you will be preparing a session of instructor-led training.

You will prepare the following documents:

- Draft content for a Running Sheet (session plan)
- Draft content for a Trainers Guide
- Visual Aids (prescribe them only - not physically create them)
- Learning and Review Activities (prescribe them only - not physically create them)

Following completion of this Learning Short-take® it would be expected that you will be able to create the following:

- A completed and typed Running Sheet
- A completed and typed Trainers Guide
- A Participant Guide
- Learning and Review Activities (physically create them)
- Visual Aids - including flipcharts
- Other logistics

In order to complete this, you will need to choose a topic of learning that can be delivered in approximately 1-2 hours.

Whether you intend to actually deliver your program or not is a secondary consideration. Remember the primary objective of this Learning Short-take® is to learn the *Instructional Design Process*.

Clearly, if you can deliver your finished product, you will have a great measure of your success and be able to build on your learnings.

Ensure that you have chosen your content area before continuing.

ABOUT
INSTRUCTIONAL
DESIGN

Part 1

About Instructional Design

What is Instructional Design?

Instructional Design is the systematic development of training materials for both trainers and participants to ensure the quality of training delivery. The person who undertakes this work is the Instructional Designer.

Instructional Design is the entire process of analysis of learning needs and the development of a delivery system to meet those needs. It includes development of instructional materials and learner activities.

Why is Instructional Design important to the training process?

Instructional Design is the key step to quality training delivery. High quality Instructional Design will maximize the success of the training program. It provides the trainer with confidence to deliver the program. Most importantly good instructional design meets the needs of all adult learners regardless of their preferred learning style.

Components of Instructional Design

Instructional Design often begins with just a glimmer of an idea of how the end training product will look. Often the Instructional Designer (who may or may not be a subject matter expert) will need to research the subject and decide on the scope of the training program.

It is assumed that solid needs analysis has been conducted to determine the learning gap of potential participants. This analysis is generally undertaken as part of the Internal Performance Consultant role, who may or may not be the same person as the Instructional Designer.

The Instructional Design process begins with writing a clear training goal and learning objectives. Then the program opening, each topic and closing of the program is written. The goal of the instructional designer is to document the program in such a way that any accomplished trainer, who has subject matter expertise, is able to pick up the instructional design materials and deliver a training program.

Instructional Design Elements

For each training program the following Instructional Design elements are expected to be developed:

- Course Outline
- Running Sheet
- Trainer's Guide
- Participant Materials
- Visual Aids

Complete Activity 1
Terms and Definition Match

Download the **ID9™ Wall Chart** from the TPC website at **www.tpc.net.au/tools**

The following terms and definitions do not match. Draw a line to match each term in the left column to the correct definition in the right column.

1

| **Presentation** | A period of time during a training day that runs between two breaks. The optimum session duration is 50 minutes for instructor-led training and 30 minutes for e-learning. |

| **Training** | A piece of content. There is no prescribed training time for this which may span from a few minutes to several sessions. |

| **Session** | Instructor-centred delivery of information and data without review or knowledge of whether the audience has learned the information, or not. |

| **Module** | Participant-centred learning, where the trainer facilitates participants to their end-goal and checks that participants are ready to apply their learning. |

1 Check your answers from the previous activity.

Presentation	Instructor-centred delivery of information and data without review or knowledge of whether the audience has learned the information, or not.

Training	Participant-centred learning, where the trainer facilitates participants to their end-goal and checks that participants are ready to apply their learning.

Session	A period of time during a training day that runs between two breaks. The optimum session duration is 50 minutes for instructor-led training and 30 minutes for e-learning.

Module	A piece of content. There is no prescribed training time for this which may span from a few minutes to several sessions.

Now update your Learning Journal (page 69)

16

▦ID9 - THE 9-STEP ID PROCESS – OVERVIEW

Part 2

ID9™ - The 9-step Instructional Design Process

 **ID9**

The following 9-step process is used to direct the flow of each training course, regardless of the delivery method. This process can be easily adapted to instructor-led training, distance learning, e-learning, or any other style of learning intervention. This model was developed by Catherine Mattiske in 1997.

OPENING PHASE	1. Welcome	Completed at the beginning of the course (once)
	2. Icebreaker	
	3. Big Picture Overview	
	4. Connect	
MODULE	5. Topic Rotation	Module structure - Repeated throughout the course, with mini-review for each module
REVIEW	6. Major Review	Measure at the end of the course
CLOSING PHASE	7. Pre-Close	Completed at the end of the course (once)
	8. Evaluation	
	9. Close	

CREATE THE
OPENING

Part 3

What is your Aim?

When it's all over - what is it you want your participants to do?

Why write an Aim?

- The aim of the course sets the purpose of attendance for participants.
- The aim helps managers understand why they are sending their staff to training.
- The aim appears on the course outline and is spoken as part of the opening Welcome by the trainer.

Guidelines

- You need to keep your course aim to one or two key sentences.
- Keep the language simple - do not use jargon or complex words.
- Use active language and specific performance outcomes - "be able to do" not "will know".
- Make it measurable – at the end of the program you must be able to assess whether participants have achieved the course aim.

Samples

- My aim is to ensure that you should be able to list five key features of the new software released.
- My aim is that participants should be able to be confident to prepare business documents using the business writing process and templates.
- My aim is that customer service staff should be able to professionally answer all calls using the standard greeting.

20

▦ ID9 Step 1 - Welcome

Structure of the Welcome

Good Morning / Good Afternoon / Hello, my name is [insert name] , my role on the team is [insert role – not life history!] . My aim is that by the end of this session, you should be able to [insert goal] .

Example: Good Morning, my name is Julie Jones, my role on the team is Team Leader of Sandwich Making. My aim is that by the end of my session, you should be able to confidently make the four basic types of sandwiches.

12 times makes perfect!

Practice your opening at least 12 times. Be flexible to change it!

- 3 times to yourself inside your head
- 2 times to yourself out loud
- 5 times to others in the office
- 2 times to someone outside of work

Ask others...

- how does it sound?
- after listening to my opening, are you interested in my session?

Complete Activity 2a
Writing the Aim

Complete Activity 2b
Welcome

Activity 2a: Writing the Aim

Activity # 1: Write your aim for your 1-2 hour session

My aim is that participants should be able to…

Activity # 2: Now imagine that you are actually speaking to your participants – make it friendly and conversational

My aim is that by the end of this session you should be able to…

Now update your Learning Journal (page 69)

© 2011, TPC – The Performance Company Pty Limited. All rights reserved.

www.tpc.net.au

Activity 2b: Welcome

Write your **Welcome!**

1

Establish credibility and why you are the person training
the course – don't give your life history!

Now update your Learning Journal (page 69)

23

▦ ID9 Step 2 - Icebreaker

What is an icebreaker?

- An icebreaker is a short activity that relaxes and engages the participants early in the process. It is a 'meet and greet' for trainer and participants.

Why create an icebreaker?

- Introduces participants to each other
- Allows the participants to be actively involved in the learning early (within 2-5 minutes of the course start)
- Creates a strategy for remembering names (handy for both the trainer and the participants)
- Creates a positive learning atmosphere
- Sets the 'pace and style' of the learning to come.

Sample # 1:
"Name Chain"

- Participants think of something starting with the first letter of their first name (adjective to describe themselves, item of clothing, type of food etc.).

- Example - Lisa Lemon or Oscar Orange

- Introduce themselves and their "thing" repeating everyone before them.

- Example - Carolyn says... This is Lisa Lemon, that's Oscar Orange and I'm Carolyn Cappuccino.

- Example - the next person, Peter, says... This is Lisa Lemon, that's Oscar Orange, that's Carolyn Cappuccino and I'm Peter Pineapple... and so on...

- Trainer goes last and repeats all participants and then adds his or her own name and their object last.

Tip # 1: There are many books with ideas for Icebreakers. Search the internet or your local bookshop to help spark ideas and creativity.

Tip # 2: Icebreakers need to be appropriate to the business culture. Ensure you match the style of Icebreaker to your audience.

Complete Activity 3
Create Your Icebreaker

Activity 3: Create your Icebreaker

1 For your sample training program, create an activity that will introduce participants to each other (i.e. get them to talk!).

When writing the icebreaker, make it **fail-proof**. It can be linked to the content, or not. Remember, it's just a quick activity to engage participants and get the ball rolling!

Now update your Learning Journal (page 69)

▦ ID9 Step 3 - Big Picture Overview

Writing Learning Objectives

Why write Learning Objectives?

- Objectives clearly establish what direction the learning is going to take.

- Objectives will help turn the needs of the business and the participants into a concrete path by focusing on exactly what is to be learnt.

- Objectives help the planning of specific activities. Everyone will know what they have to learn.

- For the instructional designer Objectives provide a road map.

- When training is being delivered, the objectives are provided with the Big Picture Overview of the program. This is especially useful for global learners.

"...that is what learning is. You suddenly understand something you've understood all your life, but in a new way."

Doris Lessing

Complete Activity 4a
Highlight Action Verbs

In the table below, highlight the words that you think are the most specific and directive for use when writing objectives

To appreciate	To know	To be aware of	To list
To be familiar with	To match	To compare	To operate
To complete	To produce	To concentrate	To realize
To construct	To recite	To contrast	To recognize
To describe	To remember	To draw	To select
To enjoy	To solve	To explain	To think critically
To grasp	To understand	To identify	To strategize

1 Check your work from the previous page. You should have highlighted all of the Action Verbs.

Use Action Verbs such as	Avoid words such as
To compare	To appreciate
To complete	To be aware of
To construct	To be familiar with
To contrast	To concentrate
To describe	To enjoy
To draw	To grasp
To explain	To know
To identify	To realize
To list	To recognize
To match	To remember
To operate	To solve
To produce	To strategize
To recite	To think critically
To select	To understand

Now update your Learning Journal (page 69)

Step 3 – Big Picture Overview – Continued

Global Learners need to see a roadmap of what will be covered in the program. As well as the learning objectives, Step 3 – Big Picture Overview also has a visual agenda. This provides an overall path of learning for all participants to follow.

It is recommended that you create a flipchart or wallchart for the Big Picture Overview so that it can be put on the wall for the duration of the training program. If you are using PowerPoint™ the learning will be limited because once the trainer moves on from the Big Picture Overview slide, participants can't refer to it throughout the program. A table of contents in your participants guide will also help the global learner navigate through the program.

Five reasons why you would create a Big Picture Overview as a flipchart...

1. So you can refer to it, when you are training
2. To take the focus off you and onto the flipchart
3. So visual learners absorb your words better
4. To give a global roadmap of where you are heading in your session
5. Can be put on the wall to help on-going learning throughout the program

In summary, the Learning Objectives, the Big Picture Overview flipchart/wallchart and the Table of Contents all provide a roadmap for participants.

Complete Activities 4b & 4c
Write Learning Objectives / Write a Big Picture Overview

1

4(b) Write Learning Objectives

4(c) Write a Big Picture Overview

Now update your Learning Journal (page 69)

■ ID9 Step 4 - Design a Connect Activity

What is a Connect Activity?

A connect activity helps participants to link course aims and objectives to the first section of content.

It is simply an opening activity designed to kick-start the learning in the training program.

Why design a Connect Activity?

1. To bridge between the Big Picture Overview and the first section of content.
2. To build rapport with the trainer and other participants.
3. To keep the flow between the opening and the content.
4. To enable the trainer to pitch the course at the appropriate level for the participants.

Sample # 1:
Expectations and Concerns

- Create a 2-sided flipchart (similar to the one shown right)
- Regroup to pairs or groups of three. Groups discuss their course expectations and any global concerns they may have. (Concerns may be about the course, outside the course, or anything that will get in the way of their learning.)
- Flipchart responses from each participant.
- At the end of the course refer back to the flipchart when conducting the evaluation phase.

Expectations	Concerns

Trainer Safe-guard:
By listening to participant's concerns you will "get any problems out in the open". Without this step the trainer reduces surprises later – possibly shown as a learning barrier or as disruptive or argumentative behavior.

Sample # 2:
Connect Activity

Things I need XXX to do for me (where XXX is the subject matter)

- Regroup to three's or four's. Groups list specific topics that they would like to cover during the course.
- 3 minutes to complete this task.
- Trainer flipcharts responses.
- Trainer goes through each response and identifies it as a topic that will be covered, won't be covered (if not, why and how participants can get this information).
- At the end of the course, mark off topics that have been covered. Ensure that participants have a 'next step' for topics not covered.

Guidelines for choosing a Connect Activity

- If participants have completed a pre-course activity the trainer will be better placed to know the expectations and concerns of the participants.

- If trainer does not confidently know each of the participants expectations for the course, then the connect activity should focus on identifying participant's expectations and concerns. (Conduct connect activity: Expectations and Concerns)

- After identifying expectations and concerns the trainer can then build on identified knowledge gaps and pitch the course at the appropriate level. (Conduct connect activity: Things I need xxx to do for me)

Complete Activity 5
Design your Connect Activity

Activity 5: Design your Connect Activity

1 For your training course, choose one of the samples provided or design your own Connect Activity for your training session. Remember it is simply an opening activity.

Now update your Learning Journal (page 69)

CREATE TRAINING MODULES

Part 4

■ID9 Step 5 - Topic Rotation

This is the most critical task in instructional design. If done well, hours of time will be saved.

If done poorly, content will continue to be added throughout the writing process, therefore wasting time and causing loss of flow of the training session.

Gather together your materials

1) Prior to starting to write you will need to **gather all materials** relevant to your training session. This may include:

- documentation.
- findings from your Analysis Phase, including pre-requisites and pre-work.
- print-outs of on-line documentation.
- reference manuals and materials.
- existing training materials.
- existing handouts.
- existing flipcharts.
- anything that *strongly* or *vaguely* relates to your topic.

2) Using post-it® notes or tags, **mark the items of content** that you want to put into your session.

3) Put the **content into priority order** - from main messages to minor messages
   - Tip: A quick way of doing this is to write on the tags - levels of priority -
     i) **Must know,**
     ii) **Should know,**
     iii) **Nice-to-know but not critical!**
   (Remember, do this from the participants perspective)

4) Write on each tag, which Learning Type the content relates to…
   - an overview of the system = why
   - to use on-the-job = why
   - step-by-step procedures = what
   - practical exercises = how
   - tips, traps and shortcuts = what-if

5) Create sections for each module of content and store in a binder or folder.

TRAP

The biggest trap for instructional designers is to launch into writing without preparing. Spend time on this preparation phase and you may save lots of time!

Step 5 – Topic Rotation – Continued

Now it is time to create each module of content. You will be working on not only the content but the learning process as well. By using the following four templates (why, what, how and what if) you will be able to work with your gathered content and create the learning process quickly and easily.

Content vs. Process

Content   The subject matter at hand. This includes all facts, data, information, theory, step-by-step processes, thoughts, ideas, concepts and suchlike.

Process   The way the content (the subject matter) will be delivered. There are a multitude of training deliver options including lecture, case study, role play, learning activities, debate, group discussion, individual work, paired activities and suchlike.

Working with Content – Tips for success

- **Work quickly.** Working with your gathered content, slot in what you can quickly and easily. Don't worry about gaps on your first draft. You can come back to these when you need to. Just remember to complete all parts.

- **Record ideas.** If you have an idea, jot it down immediately. You'll be amazed how quickly you can forget a great idea for a training process when you don't write it down!

Working with Process
- Tips for success

- **Try not to repeat Training Processes.** With so many training processes to use there is little need to repeat the way various sections of content are delivered. For example, if you use a case study for one piece of content, try to mix up the process by not using a second or third case study in the same program.

General – Tips for success

- **Look at other training courses for ideas.** If you are having difficulty completing a piece of content, a session review or any other part of the process, open up other training courses and look for ways that it has been done before. Often you don't have to reinvent the wheel!

- **Don't be tempted to leave gaps.** Remember the goal is to have a learning process that works for all types of learners. By the end of the design and development process, each learning style (visual, auditory, kinesthetic) and learning type (why, what, how, what if) should be included.

- **Get ideas from other sources.** You could also visit a toy store or bargain store for ideas. Often thinking creatively is difficult sitting at a computer, or working with a lined pad and a black pen! Go and explore!!

Design Template Overview

The following templates are provided for you to create each topic within your training program. For each topic you will create:

- the reasons why the topic is important.
- present what is covered in the topic by way of information, facts and data.
- give the participants an opportunity to see how the content works and allow practice.
- then challenge the content by asking 'what if' questions to extend the learning by adding tips, tricks and traps.

Use the following templates to assist you in writing your own training program.

Once you are confident to write each topic, you'll most likely write directly into the trainers guide. For now, simply follow the prompting questions - this will help you to build your confidence with each of the four quadrants that should be covered for each topic.

An example of each template is also provided to assist in the learning process.

Example of Module Template 1 - Write the "Why"

Sample of Completed Template: Time Management Training – Sample Section: The Time Matrix

Why is it necessary for participants to know this information?	By understanding the Time Matrix you can differentiate between urgent and non-urgent tasks and also important and unimportant tasks.
How will it help them?	It will assist you to prioritize tasks and weed out unnecessary tasks.
What do they know of this already?	This model comes from Stephen Covey's book – 7 Habits of Highly Effective People.

Group Question: Has anyone heard of Stephen Covey or seen this model before? |

Example of Module Template 2 – Write the "What"

What are the steps involved?	Define what Urgent vs. Important matters are usually visible – they have different ways to insist on action.
What is the relationship from one part to another?	Urgent matters can be important or not important. They are often urgent for other people and may be pleasant and easy for you to do...for example answering the telephone'.
	Important matters have to do with results and contribute to your long term goals – important matters can be urgent or not urgent.
What are the priorities?	Define the parts of the Time Matrix
	1. Quadrant 1 – Important & urgent
	a. Discuss examples: crisis, pressing problems, deadline driven projects
What is the order?	2. Quadrant 2 – Important but not urgent
	a. Discuss examples: prevention, relationship building, recognizing new opportunities, planning, recreation
	3. Quadrant 3 – Not important but urgent
	a. Discuss examples: interruptions, some phone calls, some mail, some reports, some meetings, pressing matters and popular activities
	4. Quadrant 4 – Not important, not urgent
	a. Discuss examples: trivia, busy work, some mail, some phone calls, timewasters, pleasant activities

"Learning is defined as a change in behavior. You haven't learned a thing until you can take action and use it."

Don Shula

Create the practice and personalization…

How can the participants be involved in the learning?	**Group Discussion** Question: What would the box look like if you spent most time in one quadrant? Answer: That quadrant would look bigger Question: Where do we probably spend most of our time now? Answer: Q1 (urgent and important) • Trainer draws box with large chunk for Q1 Question: How big would the other boxes be? Answer: Little Q2, bigger Q3 & Q4
How does this work?	
How can they try it?	
What worksheets could i create?	

1 **Results:** • Stress • Burnout • Crisis Mgmt • Always putting out fires	2
	4
3	

Group Discussion – What are the results of spending time in Q1?

Result – "Crisis & Problems"
We all have Q1 activities in our life
• Q1 consumes many people
• Dealing with deadlines and being driven to produce
• Focus on Q1 & it gets bigger & bigger
Sometimes only relief is to escape to Q4!

1 **Results:** • Short term focus 3 • Crisis mgmt • Reputation: chameleon character • See goals as pointless • Feel victimized, out of control • Shallow or broken relationships	2
	4

Group Activity 1:

Create a Time Matrix with small Quadrants 1, 2 and 4, and a large Quadrant 3 – what would the results be?

1	2
3	4
Results: • Total irresponsibility • Fired from jobs • Dependent on others for instructions on basics	

Group Activity 2:

Create a Time Matrix with large Quadrants 3 and 4, and small quadrants 1 and 2 – what would the results be?

Individual Activity 1:

Create your personal Time Matrix – actual and desired.

Examples of Module Template 4 – Write the "What if"

What can they discover themselves?	**Individual Activity – Reflective:** Reflect on your findings from the individual activity – actual vs. desired. Have participants complete their Skill Development Action Plan.
What can their learning become?	1. Write 3 things that you notice about the actual vs. desired 2. Write the one thing that you would like to change
What are the tips, tricks and traps?	3. Write the first steps on how you will implement the change
How can they add something themselves?	**Pair and Share Activity:** Share your action plan with a partner **Individual Activity:** Write barriers that may prevent you from achieving your goal. How might you overcome these barriers?

Complete Activity 6
Blank Module Template

1 – Write the "Why"

For your training program create a reason for learning...

		1 Why
Why is it necessary for participants to know this information?		
How will it help them?		
What do they know of this already?		

2 – Write the "What"

For your training program create the steps and sequence...

		What **2**
What are the steps involved?		
What is the relationship from one part to another?		
What are the priorities?		
What is the order?		

Activity 6: Continued

3 – Write the "How"

For your training program create the practice and personalization...

How 3

How can the participants be involved in the learning?	
How does this work?	
How can they try it?	
What worksheets could I create?	

4 – Write the "What If"

For your training program create the change or challenge...

4 What if

What can they discover themselves?	
What can their learning become?	
What are the tips, tricks and traps?	
How can they add something themselves?	

Now update your Learning Journal (page 69)

Module Template 5 – Learning Balance Sheet – Learning Styles – Modalities

Why create balance?

Creating balance means that regardless of which learning style and learning type a participant has, each participant is catered for. The greater the number of times a particular learning style is used then the easier the learning will be for each participant.

Example Balance Sheet – Time Management

Refer to the samples for Module Templates 1 - 4. The following shows the Learning Balance Sheet for the sample Time Management module.

What will they hear during this topic?	What will they see during this topic?	What will they do during this topic?
Trainer Guide Pair and Share Activity – discussion Group Activity – discussion	Time Matrix Flipchart Participant Guide	Participated in large and small group discussion Create personal Time Matrix Reflective Activity in What if section

What materials do you need to run this part? (e.g. handouts, visual aids, wall-charts etc)
- Stephen Covey – 7-Habits book
- Prepared flipchart – Time Matrix
- Blank Flipchart paper – to prepare variations on Time Matrix

Complete Activity 7
Blank Module Template

Activity 7: Blank Module Template

Template 5 – Learning Balance Sheet

Now check the balance of Learning Styles / Modalities for your training program.

Record in the following diagram what you have included for visual, auditory and kinesthetic.

What will they hear during this module?	What will they see during this module?	What will they do during this module?

What materials do you need to run this part? (e.g. handouts, visual aids, wall-charts etc)

Module Template 6 – Design the Topic Mini-Review

When they leave the room, how do you (their trainer), know that they know?

Rewrite your topic objective	
What proof and physical evidence will you have that the participants have met the objectives?	
Without writing an 'exam' or 'test', create a review activity that allows participants to "show you that they know"	

Now update your Learning Journal (page 69)

"Proofread carefully to see if you any words out."

Author Unknown

CREATE THE LEARNING CHECKS

Part 5 →

▦ID9 Step 6 - Major Review

What is a Major Review?

A major review is an assessment of whether participants have achieved the learning objectives, or not. It is conducted at the end of the training course or if the course is conducted over several days, the major review will be conducted at the end of each day.

Why is it important?

As a trainer you need to ensure that when participants leave the training room, they are confident to apply their new skills and knowledge in the workplace. The major review allows you to "know that they know" and gives a formal learning ending to the course.

Sample # 1:
Major Reviews

1 – True / False

- Create colored cards of statements pertaining to the course (definitions, procedures, technical information etc).

- Half of the cards have true statements on them.

- The other half has false statements on them.

- Create two cards "True" and "False".

- Put "True" "False" cards on the wall.

- Give out the statements. Participants must decide whether the statement is true or false and then put them on the wall in the correct place. Participants can help each other – but not use the trainer as a consultant.

- After all cards are in position, the trainer goes through each one, reading it aloud.

- Any incorrectly placed cards should be discussed as to why, and put on the correct side.

- All false cards can be discussed as a group, ascertaining why they are false and what the true answer is.

Sample # 2:
Step Mix

- On long pieces of colored card, write each step of a long procedure (eg. creating a table of contents, a macro, and a directory).

- Put all the steps together out of order.

- As a group, participants must put the steps in order and then put them on the wall.

Sample # 3:
Squad Challenge

- Split group into 2 teams.

- Have each team invent a "Squad Name".

- Have each squad invent the 10 hardest questions they can about any part of the course, to stump the other squad. The questioning team MUST know the answer.

- In turn the squads ask each other one question at a time.

- Award small prizes for the winning squad.

- (If you have an odd number of people – appoint an adjudicator to ask the questions, settle disputes on validity of answers and award prizes).

Sample # 4:
Questions
(as formal exercises)

Prepare a handout with the following questions:

- One thing I know about this topic is…

- I wonder…

- A word that's new to me is… it means…

- A question I have is…

- I would like more information on…

- I can use…[content] for…

Participants complete the statements. The trainer could then ask the participants to share their answers in pairs, small groups or with the whole group.

"A single conversation with a wise man is better than ten years of study."

Chinese Proverb

Complete Activity 8
Choose your Major Review

Activity 8: Choose your Major Review

Select a Major Review from the examples given, or create your own.

Using the space below list the name of the Major Review, the steps to conduct the review, the logistics required (e.g. cards, activities, markers etc) and write the Debrief Questions that will be asked following the review.

Now update your Learning Journal (page 69)

CREATE THE CLOSE

Part 6

⚏ID9 Step 7 - Pre-Close - Session Summary

You will use your session summary as a pre-close to your training. It helps participants remember the most important parts of your course. Remember to imagine they have actually been a participant in your course - so your summary is just that - a summary!

Tip: Use the least possible number of words in each point.

Complete Activity 9
Pre-Close Activity

Activity 9: Pre-Close Activity

In your training program, what were the top five key points that you want your participants to remember from your session?

1.

2.

3.

4.

5.

Now update your Learning Journal (page 69)

▦ID9 Step 8 - Evaluation

The Evaluation step is important to gauge participants reaction to the training program. Often the 'reaction evaluation' will be an evaluation form, an on-line evaluation or some type of interview questions about the training delivery and the materials presented in the program.

In this step, you will be following your organizations process for evaluation.

Complete Activity 10
Conduct an Interview!

Conduct an interview and use resource materials to find out the evaluation process that you need to use at the end of each session. Sources of this may be your intranet, your manager, other trainers or your own prior knowledge. List your findings.

Now update your Learning Journal (page 69)

ID9 Step 9 - Close

1

Like the best productions, musicals, plays, and concerts - you need to close with gusto and pizzazz and create finality that tells your participants "It's over!" You will need to leave them with a parting thought, motivating quote or relevant story (with a point and a benefit to them).

Sample # 1:
Close

For example: (for customer service, asset management etc.)

May I leave you with a thought from a professor of management at the University of New Orleans and the author of How to Win customers and keep them for life.

"Don't ever make the mistake of thinking of buildings, computers, consultants, or even employees as you company's greatest assets. Every company's greatest assets are its customers, because without customers there is no company. It's that simple."

The reason why our team does what it does is to make the company grow. With this growth we can increase the number of customers and have them delighted with our service. The knock-on effect is we, the employees are happy and the shareholders are happy. I hope that you can see from my session, this system really has tremendous opportunity for growing the company. Thank you.

Complete Activity 11
Write your Close

Use books of quotes or stories from newspapers to help you in creating your close.

Now update your Learning Journal (page 69)

Your planning is complete!

"Learning is not attained by chance,
it must be sought for with ardor
and attended to with diligence."

Abigail Adams

CREATE
MATERIALS

Part 7

Create final documentation

Sample Running Sheet

Sample Trainer's Guide

If you choose to complete your sample training project so that it can be delivered to participants, then you would create the following instructional design documentation.

- A completed and typed Running Sheet (in your standard corporate format).

- A completed and typed Trainers Guide (in your standard corporate format).

- A Participant Guide (in your standard corporate format).

- Learning and Review Activities (physically create them).

- Visual Aids including flipcharts, PowerPoint™ presentation.

- Other logistics (such as markers, notepads, music, administration documentation etc).

"Success will never be a big step in the future, success is a small step taken just now."

Jonatan Martensson

Now update your Learning Journal (page 69)

Section 2

LEARNING JOURNAL

The Learning Journal is used throughout the Learning Short-take® process to record your key learnings, hot tips and things to remember.

Update your Learning Journal at anytime throughout the Learning Short-take® process. Ensure you complete your Learning Journal after you finish each activity. Then turn back to the Participant Guide to continue your learning.

Learning Journal

As you work through this Learning Short-take®, make detailed notes on this page of the lessons you have learned and any useful skill areas. For each lesson or refresher point think about how you could further develop this skill. Your coach will want to discuss these with you in your Skill Development Action Planning meeting.

"…that is what learning is.
You suddenly understand something you've understood all your life, but in a new way."

Doris Lessing

"Anyone who stops learning is old, whether at twenty or eighty."

Henry Ford

"The wise do at once what the fool does later."
Baltasar Gracian (1601-58), Spanish Jesuit priest and author.

Learning or Idea	Action to be taken	Result Expected

Learning Journal - continued

Learning or Idea	Action to be taken	Result Expected

"Anyone who stops learning is old, whether at twenty or eighty."
Henry Ford

Learning or Idea	Action to be taken	Result Expected

2

2

"In real life the greatest heroes
are often found among the most
ordinary people.
Do not wait for extraordinary
circumstances to do good;
try to use ordinary situations."

Jean Paul Richter

Section 3

SKILL DEVELOPMENT ACTION PLAN

Your Skill Development Action Plan is the last Step in the Learning Short-take® process. After you have completed the Participant Guide and all Activities update your Learning Journal then complete this section.

Skill Development
Action Plan

This is the most important part of the program - your individual Skill Development Action Plan.

You need to complete this plan before meeting with your manager or prior to on-going coaching. You will discuss it in detail with your manager or coach as he or she will ensure that you have everything you need to complete the tasks and activities.

Once you have completed your **Skill Development Action Plan** schedule a meeting time with your manager or coach to review your plan. Take your participant guide and all other documentation received during the training course to this meeting.

Remember - you have committed to your **Skill Development Action Plan**, and need to make time to complete your tasks!

"The mind, once stretched by a new idea, never regains its original dimensions."

Oliver Wendell Holmes

"Whatever you can do or dream you can - begin it. Boldness has genius, power and magic."

Johann Wolfgang von Goethe

"Imagination is the eye of the soul."
Joseph Joubert (1754-1824)

Task or activity (Be specific)	Measure (this will help you to know you have achieved it)	Date (Be specific)
Reflect on your Learning Journal. Transfer action items that you can apply to your job. Ensure that you include some 'stretch goals' and also a blend of short, medium and long term goals.	Apart from you, who else is needed to assist you in achieving your goal.	Be specific. A general date such as 'Quarter 1', 'August', or 'by end of year' is vague and more likely to result in not achieving your target. Be specific – e.g. 22nd November.

Ideas for discussion with my manager

Ideas

Congratulations!

Meet with your Manager/Coach to discuss your
Skill Development Action Plan.

3

"You gain strength, courage, and confidence
by every experience in which you really stop to
look fear in the face...

The danger lies in refusing to face the fear,
in not daring to come to grips with it...

You must make yourself succeed every time.
You must do the thing you think you cannot do."

Eleanor Roosevelt

extra

QUICK
REFERENCE

This Quick Reference provides you with a summary of key concepts,
models and reference material from Learning Short-takes®.
We have also included some quotations to ponder.

Use this section as a quick reference to keep your learning active.

4

" Anyone who stops learning is old, whether at twenty or eighty. "

Henry Ford

Instructional Design

4

Instructional Design is the systematic development of training materials for both trainers and participants to ensure the quality of training delivery.

The person who undertakes this work is the Instructional Designer.

©2011, TPC - The Performance Company Pty Limited. All rights reserved.
www.tpc.net.au
83

Instructional Design Elements

4

For each training program the following Instructional Design elements should be developed:

- Course Outline
- Running Sheet
- Trainer's Guide
- Participant Materials
- Visual Aids

ID9™ - The 9-Step Instructional Design Process

4

MATTISKE'S
9STEP INSTRUCTIONAL
DESIGN PROCESS

OPENING PHASE	1. Welcome	Completed at the beginning of the course (once)
	2. Icebreaker	
	3. Big Picture Overview	
	4. Connect	
MODULE	5. Topic Rotation	Module structure – Repeated throughout the course, with mini-review for each module
REVIEW	6. Major Review	Measure at the end of the course
CLOSING PHASE	7. Pre-Close	Completed at the end of the course (once)
	8. Evaluation	
	9. Close	

4

**" When it's all over -
what is it you want
your participants
to do? "**

Step 1 - Welcome

4

The welcome should include:

- Your name
- The course aim

Structure of the Course Aim:

> By the end of this training program participants should be able to [behavioral goal] so that [benefit to participants and or the organization]

Step 2 - Icebreaker

4

An icebreaker is a short activity that relaxes and engages the participants early in the process.

It is a 'meet and greet' for trainer and participants.

Step 3 - Big Picture Overview

Learning Objectives clearly establish what direction the learning is going to take and focus the needs of the business and the participants into a concrete learning path.

The Agenda assists global learners to see a snapshot of the entire course content linked to the course aim.

Behavioral Learning Objectives

4

Use Action Verbs such as	Avoid words such as
To compare	To appreciate
To complete	To be aware of
To construct	To be familiar with
To contrast	To concentrate
To describe	To enjoy
To draw	To grasp
To explain	To know
To identify	To realize
To list	To recognize
To match	To remember
To operate	To feel confident with
To point to	To think critically
To recite	To understand
To select	To be ready to

Step 4 -
Design a Connect Activity

A connect activity is an introductory activity that link course aims and objectives to the first section of content.

Step 5 - Topic Rotation

4

What will they hear during this topic?	What will they see during this topic?	What will they do during this topic?

Step 6 - Major Review

A major review is an assessment of whether participants have achieved the learning objectives, or not.

It is conducted at the end of the training course or if the course is conducted over several days, the major review will be conducted at the end of each day.

Step 7 - Pre-Close Session Summary

4

A summary of key points.

Helps participants remember the most important parts of your course.

Step 8 - Evaluation

The Evaluation step is important to gauge participants reaction to the training program.

" One of the great mistakes is to judge policies and programs by their intentions rather than their results. "

Milton Friedman

Step 9 - Close

4

Create finality that tells your participants "It's over!"

Leave them with a parting thought, motivating quote or relevant story.

Participants remember best what they hear first and last.

NEXT STEPS

Congratulations! You have now completed this Learning Short-take® title. The entire list of Learning Short-takes® can be found on the TPC website.

In this section we have suggested Learning Short-take® titles for you that will build your learning. You may order these Learning Short-takes® online at www.tpc.net.au or from your bookstores.

Adult Learning Principles 1
Understanding the Ways Adults Learn

Learning Short-take® Outline

Adult Learning Principles 1 combines self-study with realistic workplace activities for trainers, educators, facilitators and managers to develop skills and knowledge in the principles of adult learning. It will add adult learning techniques to your 'grab bag' of learning design tools for improved learning outcomes. After evaluation of your current approach to learning design, you will learn to develop new and innovative strategies to engage learners at every level. Significantly increasing participant retention and training results **Adult Learning Principles 1** will fuel your confidence in designing successful training workshops and e-Learning every time.

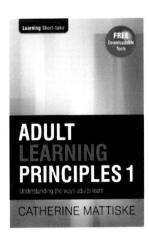

The principles of adult learning work on the basis that we all learn differently, and the way we like to receive and interpret information varies from person to person. Trainers and facilitators who use a combination of adult learning principles to provide balance in their programs increase the chances of keeping all participants focused and engaged throughout the learning process. **Adult Learning Principles 1** will assist you in building a good mix of adult learning styles which is critical in ensuring learning, thorough participant retention and workplace application.

Adult Learning Principles 1 includes the **Adult Learning Principles Quick Reference Wall Chart**, provided as a free downloadable tool.

Learning Objectives

- Successfully match adult learning terms with definitions.

- Determine your personal Learning Style preference.

- List and give working examples of three Adult Learning Principles – Global vs Specific, Learning Styles and Learning Types.

- Develop strategies and ideas to link Adult Learning Principles with Instructional Design.

Course Content

- Part 1: Understanding Adult Learners

- Part 2: Adult Learning Principle 1 - Global vs Specific Learners

- Part 3: Adult Learning Principle 2 - Learning Style - Modalities

- Part 4: Adult Learning Principle 3 - Learning Types - The 4Mat System

Adult Learning Principles 2
Blending Interaction with Measurement

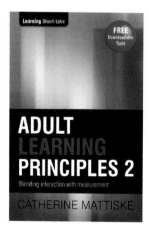

Course Content

- Part 1: Understanding ROI
- Part 2: Measurement Myths
- Part 3: Kirkpatrick's Model
- Part 4: Measuring through Review
- Part 5: Bringing it Together

Learning Short-take® Outline

Adult Learning Principles 2 combines self-study with realistic workplace activities to develop skills in learning measurement. Building on Adult Learning Principles 1, this Learning Short-take® examines the importance of Return on Investment (ROI) in training and explores common myths around learning measurement. For trainers, educators, facilitators and managers the library of training activities will allow you to develop new and innovative strategies to assess learning during workshops, training programs and e-Learning sessions.

In the world of training and development, the subject of measuring ROI is discussed frequently. Organizations everywhere are searching for the perfect measurement system to link human resource capability with the business strategy. To achieve this result, it is important to understand how learning can be effectively measured in the classroom. It is during the training itself that we have the first opportunity to observe learning transfer taking place.

Adult Learning Principles 2 provides a library of 18 training activities that can be used to measure learning during training courses. It also includes the **Training Review Analysis** tool, provided as a free download.

Learning Objectives

- Explain the importance of ROI (Return on Investment) in training.
- Identify common myths about measuring training in the classroom.
- Explain Kirkpatrick's Learning Evaluation Model.
- Explain the value of Review as a solid training measurement
- Describe the various types of Reviews.
- Identify and explain the different levels of Review.
- Create a Skill Development Action Plan.

Adult Learning Principles 3
Advanced Adult Learning Principles

Learning Short-take® Outline

Adult Learning Principles 3 combines self-study with realistic workplace activities to build advanced knowledge of adult learning principles. Building on Adult Learning Principles 1 and 2, it explores three sophisticated principles of adult learning: Multiple Intelligences, Whole Brain Learning and Metacognitive Reflection. **Adult Learning Principles 3** is designed for educators, trainers and facilitators who work in instructor-led training, e-Learning, distance learning, self-study and other types of learning interventions.

The reliance on just a few training approaches may be a combination of trainer "comfort" and organizational expectations. Often, corporate training represents a school-like environment: lectures followed with an activity. With increasing pressure on training departments to reduce training session duration and convert instructor led training to e-learning, trainers must adopt new ways of delivering learning. This Learning Short-take® will provide a plethora of new ideas and refuel the way you design learning.

Adult Learning Principles 3 includes the **Multiple Intelligence Quick Reference Card**, provided as a free downloadable tool.

Learning Objectives

- Explain the value of using a balanced adult learning approach.
- List the characteristics of left brain dominance vs. right brain dominance.
- Use the Brain Dominance theory to analyze and make improvements to an existing training program.
- List the Multiple Intelligences.
- Analyze an existing training program and suggest improvements to maximize the Multiple Intelligence Balance.
- Define metacognitive reflection and be able to implement learning and review activities using this training method.
- Create a Skill Development Action Plan.

Course Content

- Part 1: Whole Brain Learning
  - Brain Dominance
  - Assessing Hemispheric Dominance

- Part 2: Multiple Intelligences
  - Logical-Mathematical Intelligence
  - Musical Intelligence
  - Bodily-Kinesthetic Intelligence
  - Visual/Spatial Intelligence
  - Interpersonal Intelligence
  - Intrapersonal Intelligence
  - Naturalist Intelligence
  - Existential Intelligence

- Part 3: The Metacognitive Process
  - Strategies for Developing Metacognitive Behaviors
  - Journal Writing

CPSIA information can be obtained
at www.ICGtesting.com
Printed in the USA
LVIW021447190413
330046LV00001B

* 9 7 8 1 9 2 1 5 4 7 0 6 5 *